MACMILLAN READERS

PRE-INTERMEDIATE LEVEL

FRANCES HODGSON BURNETT

The Secret Garden

Retold by Rachel Bladon

macmillan education

Macmillan Readers is a series of engaging narrative texts designed to stimulate learners while enhancing their language skills, building literacy and boosting reading confidence. Through captivating stories and fascinating cultural themes, learners will explore a diversity of scenarios that foster vocabulary expansion, comprehension skills and a lifelong love of reading.

The right reader at every stage
Tailored to each learner's stage of language proficiency, our six levels feature text adapted to match the skill level. With controlled vocabulary and grammar, learners can read freely and immerse themselves in the story. When more challenging words are introduced, either the text will provide sufficient context to aid understanding or a full explanation will be provided in the Glossary.

Readers for all, anywhere, anytime
Macmillan Readers are perfect for shared, guided and independent reading. Whether in traditional print, immersive audio or the convenient eBook, Macmillan Readers are equally effective for in-class activities, paired discussions or solo reading at home or on the move.

Reading for pleasure, knowledge and well-being
Regular reading and reading for pleasure:

- increases reading confidence, benefiting all literacy skills, not just reading.
- reinforces and enriches vocabulary, providing a variety of contexts.
- expands general knowledge.
- supports concentration, inner reflection and well-being.

Macmillan Readers will inspire a love for reading in English while nurturing essential language skills. Unlock new worlds, expand horizons and embark on an adventure in English!

(NOTE: *While the content of Macmillan Readers is evaluated for age suitability, we kindly remind parents and teachers that they are ultimately responsible for determining whether a particular book is appropriate for their child or student.)*

Contents

A Note About the Author

Frances Hodgson Burnett wrote *The Secret Garden* in 1911, and it is probably the most famous of all her books. In her lifetime Frances wrote more than forty books, for adults as well as children. However, she is most well-known for her children's stories.

Frances Eliza Hodgson (Fanny) was born in 1849 in Manchester, England. When she was young, her father died, and her family became very poor. At that time in England, poor people lived very hard lives. The Hodgson family had a relative who lived in the United States, so in 1865 they decided to move to Knoxville, Tennessee. The family liked living in Tennessee, but they did not get any help from their relatives. They were still terribly poor and when Frances was 18 years old, her mother died.

After that, Frances had to look after her brothers and sisters. She started writing for American magazines, to make some money. Her first story was published in 1868, and slowly, people started to realize that she was a very good writer. In 1873, she married Dr Swan Burnett. From then on, she wrote under her husband's name, and it was as Frances Hodgson Burnett that she became very famous.

Her first novel, *That Lass O'Lowrie's*, was published in 1877. It was about poor people in Manchester. And in 1886, her children's book *Little Lord Fauntleroy* was published. It immediately became loved all around the world and sold more than half a million copies.

From the mid-1890s, Frances Hodgson Burnett lived mainly in England. She wrote the play *The Lady of Quality* in 1896, and the children's book *A Little Princess* in 1905. In 1909, she moved back to Long Island, in the United States, where she wrote *The Secret Garden*. Frances Hodgson Burnett died in Plandome, New York, in 1924.

A Note About This Story

This story starts in the early 1900s. At the beginning of the story, Mary Lennox comes from India to live in Yorkshire in England. India was still part of the British Empire[1] at that time and lots of British people lived and worked there. They always had Indian servants[2], and sometimes they did not treat their servants well. The British thought that Indian people were less important than themselves.

When Mary comes to England from India, she does not know how to be polite or kind to people. Because her parents never had time for her, she is lonely and angry. She does not know how to make friends. However, at Misselthwaite Manor[3] in Yorkshire, she meets the maid Martha and her brother Dickon. Martha and Dickon are poor but happy, because they come from a loving home. Mary also meets Colin, a boy who is also unloved. Like Mary, Colin feels angry and lonely.

One morning, Mary discovers a hidden garden where no one has been for ten years. She and her friends decide to care for it. And as the garden starts to grow and bloom when spring comes, the children too begin to come alive. At the same time, Mary learns how to be a good person.

The Secret Garden is a magical story about children who find new happiness through the simple joys of nature. Nearly a hundred years later, it is still one of the most well-loved children's books ever written.

The People in This Story

Mary Lennox

Master Craven

Colin Craven

Martha Sowerby

Dickon Sowerby

Ben Weatherstaff

Mrs Medlock

1

Mary Comes to England

Mary Lennox was born in India. When she was nine years old, her mother and father died of cholera.[4] Mary did not miss her mother very much when she was gone. She had not seen or spoken to her very much when she was alive.

Mary's mother had not wanted a child at all. She had been very beautiful, and she had only been interested in going to parties and meeting people. Mary's father was always busy with his work, too. So when Mary was born, a servant looked after her. Her mother told the servant to make sure that Mary did not cry or make too much noise. So the servant always gave Mary whatever she asked for and Mary quickly became a very difficult and selfish[5] little girl.

Mary was a plain-looking child, too. She had a thin little face and body, and she always looked cross.

Because Mary was such a selfish little girl, she only really thought about herself. She wanted to know who would look after her now that her parents had died. She hoped they would let her do what she wanted.

At first, Mary went to stay with a family called the Crawfords, in India. But Mary was so disagreeable[6] that none of the Crawford children wanted to play with her. After she had been there for a week, one of the Crawfords' little boys told her that she was going to go back to England.

'You are going to live with your uncle,' the boy said. 'He lives in a great big old house in the country. He's so cross, he won't let people come and see him. And no one would want to see him anyway. He's a hunchback[7], and he's horrible.'

'I don't believe you,' said Mary, and she turned her back and put her fingers in her ears.

But that night, Mrs Crawford told her that she would sail to England in a few days' time. She said that Mary would live with her uncle, Mr Archibald Craven, at Misselthwaite Manor in Yorkshire.

'Mary is such a plain child – and so disagreeable,' said Mrs Crawford afterwards. 'And yet her mother was so pretty, and so delightful[8]. Perhaps if Mary's mother had spent a little more time with her, she might have learned to be delightful too. But most people didn't even know that she had a child.'

When Mary arrived in England, she was met in London by Mr Craven's housekeeper[9], Mrs Medlock. Mrs Medlock took Mary up to Yorkshire by train. Mrs Medlock was a large woman, with very red cheeks and sharp black eyes. She was not a very patient woman, and she was not interested in young children.

Mary did not like Mrs Medlock at all. In the train, she sat as far as possible from her, looking bored and unhappy. Her black dress made her look more yellow than ever, and her hair hung down messily[10] underneath her hat.

'I've never seen such a spoilt[11]-looking child in my life,' Mrs Medlock thought to herself.

After a while, the housekeeper began to talk to Mary in a hard, sharp voice.

'I suppose I had better tell you something about where you are going to,' she said. She waited for Mary to reply, but Mary said nothing at all. 'It's a very strange place,' Mrs Medlock went on. 'It's big and grand, of course, but very gloomy[12]. The house is six hundred years old, and it's on the edge of the moor[13]. There are nearly a hundred rooms, with pictures and beautiful old furniture, but most of them are shut up and locked. There's a big park around the house, with gardens and big trees. But there's nothing else,' she ended suddenly.

Mary had begun to listen. It all sounded very different from India, and she liked new things. But she tried to look as if she wasn't interested.

'I certainly don't know why you're going there,' Mrs Medlock went on. 'Mr Craven's not going to look after you, I'm sure about that. He doesn't care about anyone. He has a crooked[14] back. That gave him a bad start in life. He was a cross young man and he didn't do any good until he got married.'

Mary looked up. She had not known that Mr Craven was married, and she was surprised. Mrs Medlock saw that Mary was interested, and went on talking.

'His wife was a sweet, pretty thing. He'd have done anything for her. People said she only married him for his money, but that's not true. Then she died, and he became stranger than ever. He doesn't care about anyone now. Most of the time he goes away. But when he is at Misselthwaite, he shuts himself up and won't see anyone. You probably won't see him at all. And there won't be anyone to talk to you. You will have to play on your own. I'll tell you which rooms you can go into. But you mustn't go walking all around the house. Mr Craven wouldn't like it.'

Listening to Mrs Medlock did not make Mary feel very happy. A house with a hundred rooms, nearly all shut up and locked. A man with a crooked back who shut himself up too! She stared out of the window of the train and that made her feel even more gloomy, because it had started to rain. She watched the grey sky grow heavier and heavier, and then she fell asleep.

When Mary woke up, she and Mrs Medlock ate some lunch, but she soon fell asleep once more. When she woke again, the train had stopped at a station and Mrs Medlock was shaking her.

'Wake up!' she said. 'We've arrived.'

Mary watched as Mrs Medlock collected up their bags. She did not help, because she was not used to helping. In India, servants had always done everything for her. Then Mary followed Mrs Medlock through the station and outside, where a carriage[15] was waiting. Mary climbed in, and they set off. She felt curious[16] about where they were going.

'What is a moor?' she asked suddenly.

'Look out of the window and you'll see,' Mrs Medlock replied.

Mary looked out of the window. They were on a rough road, with bushes and low-growing things on both sides. Beyond that, all she could see was darkness stretching out all around them. The wind was making a strange low sound.

'Is it the sea?' Mary asked.

'No,' replied Mrs Medlock. 'And it's not fields or mountains, either. It's just miles and miles of wild land. The only things that grow there are heather[17] and gorse[18]. And the only things that live there are wild ponies[19] and sheep.'

'It sounds just like the sea,' said Mary.

'That's the sound of the wind blowing through the bushes,' said Mrs Medlock. 'I think it's a dull, wild place. But plenty of people like it.'

They drove on through the darkness, until at last Mary saw a light in the distance. Mrs Medlock saw it at the same time.

'We're nearly there now,' she said.

At last the carriage pulled up in front of a long, low-built house. Most of it was in darkness, but there was a light in one of the upstairs rooms. Mary followed Mrs Medlock through the large wooden front door into the hall. It was a very large room, and the walls were covered with paintings of people who had lived a long time ago. But it was so dark in the hall that Mary found it quite frightening to look at the paintings. She suddenly felt very small and lost.

'I'll take you to your room now,' said Mrs Medlock. She led Mary up some stairs, down a long corridor[20], up some more stairs and along two more corridors. Then she opened a door into a room. There was a fire burning in the room, and there was some dinner on the table.

'Here you are,' said Mrs Medlock. 'You will live here, and in the room next door. And you must stay in these rooms. Don't forget that!'

And that is how Mary began her life at Misselthwaite Manor.

2

Robin Redbreast[21]

When Mary opened her eyes in the morning, there was a young servant girl cleaning out the fireplace in her room. Mary lay and watched her for a few moments and then looked around the room. It was not like a child's room at all. It was strange and gloomy, and there were no toys or books.

There was a large window, and through it Mary could see a huge area of land climbing up into the distance. There were no trees on it, and it looked like an endless, purple sea.

'What is that?' Mary asked, pointing out of the window.

'That's the moor,' said Martha, the young servant girl, standing up and looking out. 'Do you like it?'

'No,' answered Mary. 'I hate it.'

'That's because you're not used to it,' Martha said cheerfully, turning back to her work. 'Wait till spring and summer, when the gorse and heather are in flower. Then it smells like honey. The sky looks so high, and the bees and the birds make such a noise humming[22] and singing. Then you'll like it.'

Martha was a round, red-cheeked, cheerful-looking person. She spoke with a strong Yorkshire accent[23], and Mary listened to her in surprise. She was not at all like the servants Mary had

had in India. They always did everything Mary wanted and if they disobeyed[24] her she hit them in the face. Martha did not talk to Mary like she was an important person. But Martha was quite a strong-looking girl and Mary thought that if she hit Martha, Martha might possibly hit her back.

'Are you going to be my servant?' Mary asked Martha, in her proud, unfriendly way.

'I'm Mrs Medlock's servant,' said Martha. 'But I shall clean your room, and bring you your meals.'

'Who is going to dress me?' asked Mary.

Martha sat up and stared at Mary.

'Can't you dress yourself?' she asked, amazed.

'No,' answered Mary, crossly. 'I've never dressed myself. My servants always did it.'

'Well,' said Martha. 'It's time you learnt to do it yourself.'

Mary began to feel horribly lonely and very far away from everything she knew. Suddenly she threw herself down on the bed and started to cry so loudly that Martha felt a little frightened. She also felt quite sorry[25] for Mary. She went to the bed and stood next to her.

'Eh, you mustn't cry like that,' she said. 'I'm sorry, Miss. Do stop crying.'

Mary slowly stopped crying and became quiet. Martha looked relieved[26].

'It's time for you to get up now,' the maid said. 'Your breakfast is ready next door. If you get out of bed, I'll help you put your clothes on.'

Martha chattered[27] away as she helped Mary to get dressed. Mary listened coldly at first, but slowly she began to be interested.

'There are twelve children in our house, and there's never enough food for all of them,' said Martha. 'They run and play on the moor all day. Mother says the fresh air of the moor fattens them up. She thinks they must eat grass, just like the ponies! Our Dickon, he's twelve years old and he's found a young pony to play with.'

'Where did he get it?' asked Mary.

'He found it on the moor with its mother when it was little,' Martha told her. 'He started to make friends with it and give it bits of bread. And now it follows him around and lets him get on its back. Dickon's a kind boy and the animals like him.'

Mary had always thought it would be nice to have a pet animal. So she started to feel a little interested in Dickon. And that was a strange feeling for her. She had only ever been interested in herself before.

When Mary went into the room next door, there was a large breakfast laid out on the table. But she had never eaten much, and when Martha put a plate in front of her she pushed it away.

'I don't want it,' she said.

'Don't want it?' cried Martha, shocked. 'If our children were here, they'd eat all this up in five minutes.'

'Why?' asked Mary coldly.

'Why?' repeated Martha. 'Because they've never had full stomachs in their lives. They're as hungry as foxes[28].'

Mary didn't know what it was like to be hungry. She drank some tea and ate a little bit of toast.

'Now put some warm clothes on and go out and play,' said Martha. 'It'll be good for you.'

'Who will go with me?' Mary asked.

Martha stared at her.

'You'll go by yourself,' she answered. 'You'll have to learn to play by yourself, like other children. Our Dickon goes off on the moor by himself for hours and hours. That's how he made friends with the pony. There are sheep on the moor that know him, and birds come and eat out of his hand. He always saves a bit of bread for them.'

Mary thought for a moment. There wouldn't be ponies or sheep in the garden, but there might be birds. And they would probably be different from the ones in India. It might be interesting to look at them. And there was certainly nothing to do indoors.

Martha found Mary's coat and hat and a pair of little boots, and showed her the way downstairs.

'If you go that way, you'll come to the gardens,' she said, pointing to a gate. 'There are lots of flowers there in the summer, but they're rather bare[29] right now.' After a moment, she added, 'One of the gardens is locked up. No one has been in it for ten years.'

'Why?' asked Mary. Normally she didn't like to show that she was interested. But this sounded very strange.

'Mr Craven had it shut when his wife died so suddenly. He won't let anyone go inside. It was her garden. He locked the door and buried[30] the key.'

At that moment, they heard a bell ring.

'Mrs Medlock's calling me,' said Martha, and she went inside.

After Martha had gone, Mary went out into the gardens. There were wide lawns[31], trees and flower beds, and a large pool with an old grey fountain[32] in the middle. But the flower beds were bare, and the fountain was not playing. Mary could not stop thinking about the locked garden. 'What would it look like now?' she wondered. 'Would the flowers still be alive?'

At the end of the path Mary was following, she saw a long wall with a green door in it. She went through the door and found herself in a walled garden. There were some fruit trees growing against the wall, and a few beds of winter vegetables, but otherwise it was bare. A doorway led from there into another walled garden, and there were several more beyond. Mary walked through the gardens until she came to an orchard[33] – a garden full of fruit trees. The walls seemed to go beyond the orchard, as if there was a garden on the other side. But there was no door in the orchard wall. Mary could see the tops of trees above the wall. As she looked up she saw a bird with a bright red breast sitting on top of one of the trees. Suddenly he started to sing his winter song, as if he had just noticed her and was calling to her.

The bird's cheerful little song gave Mary a pleasant feeling. The big closed house and bare moor had made Mary feel as if she was all alone in this world. But this little bird almost made her smile. She listened to him until he flew away. Then she started to walk back towards the first walled garden. She kept thinking about the locked garden, probably because she had nothing else to do. Then she thought of the little bird with the red breast, and suddenly she stopped.

'I think he was on a tree in the secret garden,' she said to herself. 'I'm sure he was. There was a wall around the place, and there was no door.'

She had reached the door to the first walled garden by now. As she came into it, she noticed that an old man was now digging[34] in the corner. He looked up as she came in, and nodded at her. He had an unfriendly face, and did not look pleased to see her. She walked over and stood watching him in her cold little way. He did not look up again, so at last she spoke to him.

'I can't find the door into the other garden,' she said.

'What garden?' the man said in a rough voice. He stopped digging for a moment.

'The one behind the orchard,' answered Mary. 'There were trees there. I saw the tops of them. A bird with a red breast was sitting on one of them, and he sang.'

To Mary's surprise, the gardener suddenly smiled. He turned around and whistled[35] softly. Then a wonderful thing happened. The bird with the red breast came flying over to them, and landed on the earth near the gardener's foot.

'Here he is,' laughed the old man. 'Where have you been, you cheeky thing?'

The bird looked up at him with his soft black eye. He didn't seem at all frightened. He hopped[36] about, looking for insects.

'What kind of bird is he?' Mary asked.

'Don't you know?' the old man replied. 'He's a robin redbreast. They're the friendliest birds of all. I've known this one since he was a baby. His brothers and sisters flew away, and he was lonely.'

Mary went a little nearer to the robin and looked at him very hard.

'I'm lonely,' she said. She suddenly realized[37] that this was one of the things that made her feel so cross all the time.

The old gardener stared at her for a minute.

'Are you the little girl from India?' he asked.

Mary nodded. 'What is your name?' she asked.

'Ben Weatherstaff,' he answered. Then he said, with a little laugh, 'I'm lonely too. That robin's the only friend I've got.'

'I don't have any friends at all,' said Mary. 'I've never played with anyone.'

'You're probably a little bit like me,' said old Ben Weatherstaff. 'Neither of us are good-looking. And we're both as cross as we look. I expect you've probably got a horrible temper[38] like me, too.'

No one had ever talked to Mary like that before.

'Do I really look as cross as Ben Weatherstaff?' she thought to herself. 'And do I have a horrible temper?' She felt rather uncomfortable.

Suddenly they both looked up. The robin had flown onto an apple tree close to Mary, and had started singing. Ben Weatherstaff laughed.

'He's decided to make friends with you,' said Ben. 'He likes you!'

Mary moved carefully towards the tree, and looked up.

'Would you make friends with me?' she asked the robin. But she did not say it in her hard little voice. She spoke softly and gently.

At that moment, the robin stopped singing, shook his wings and flew away.

'He has flown over the wall!' cried Mary, watching him. 'He has flown across the orchard into the locked garden.'

'He lives there,' said old Ben. 'He lives there, among the rose-trees.'

'Are there rose-trees? I'd like to see them,' said Mary. 'Where is the door to the garden?'

Ben suddenly became cold and unfriendly once more.

'There isn't a door,' he said roughly. 'There was ten years ago, but there isn't now. Now go and play. I've got to work.'

And he picked up his spade[39] and walked away. He didn't even look at Mary or say goodbye.

3

Mary Finds the Key

For the first week or two, every day was exactly the same for Mary. There was nothing for her to do indoors, so after breakfast she went out into the gardens. The wind, which blew down from the moor, was strong and cold. Mary had to run to keep herself warm. She did not know that this was good for her. She did not know that the fresh air was making her thin body stronger and bringing some red colour into her cheeks.

For the first few days, Mary had not eaten the breakfast Martha brought her. But one morning, after several days of running around outside, she woke up with a strange feeling. She realized that for the first time in her life she felt hungry. When Martha brought her breakfast that day, she picked up her spoon and started eating it. And she went on eating until it had all gone.

'The fresh air of the moor is making you hungry,' said Martha. 'If you play outside every day you'll get bigger and stronger.'

'I don't play,' said Mary. 'I have nothing to play with.'

'Nothing to play with!' cried Martha. 'Our children play with sticks and stones. They just run about and shout and look at things.'

Mary did not shout, but she did look at things. She walked round and round the gardens and the park. Sometimes she looked for Ben Weatherstaff, but he was always too busy or too unfriendly to talk to her.

There was one place that Mary went to more than anywhere else. It was the long walk outside the kitchen gardens. The walls there were covered with ivy[40]. In one part the ivy was so thick it looked as if no one had cut it for years. One morning,

Mary was looking at the ivy and thinking about this, when she heard a loud twitter[41] up above. She looked up and saw the robin sitting on a treetop.

'Oh, it's you!' Mary laughed happily. The first time Mary had seen the robin, he had been sitting on a treetop and she had been standing in the orchard. But looking at him now, she realized that he was sitting on top of the same tree. She looked up at the ivy-covered wall.

'The robin's in the secret garden again,' she said to herself. 'And this must be the back wall of the garden.'

Mary ran up to the green door she had gone through the first morning. Then she ran down through the kitchen gardens into the orchard, and looked up above the wall. Sure enough, there was the robin sitting on the treetop. Mary walked along, looking closely at the orchard wall, but there was no door. Then she ran back out to the long ivy-covered wall and looked at that side carefully, too. But there was no door there either.

'It's very strange,' she said to herself. 'Ben Weatherstaff said there was no door, and he's right. But there must have been a door ten years ago, because Mr Craven buried the key.'

Mary began to feel very interested in the secret garden. One evening after supper, she sat down in front of the fire and asked Martha a question.

'Why did Mr Craven hate the garden?' she said.

'Are you still thinking about that garden?' said Martha. She came and sat down next to Mary. It was a windy night. There was a low roaring noise as the wind rushed around the house. It beat against the walls and windows.

'Mrs Medlock says no one should talk about it,' Martha said. 'If it wasn't for that garden, Mr Craven wouldn't be like he is. It was Mrs Craven's garden, and she just loved it. They used to look after it themselves. None of the gardeners were allowed to go in it. Mr and Mrs Craven sat there for hours and hours, reading and talking. There was an old tree with a big branch[42], and Mrs Craven liked to sit on the branch. But one day when she was sitting on it, the branch broke. She fell to the ground and she was hurt very badly. The next day she died. The doctors thought Mr Craven would go mad and die too. And that's why he hates the garden. No one has been inside since, and no one is allowed to talk about it.'

All at once Mary felt sorry for Mr Craven. It was the first time she had ever felt sorry for anyone before, and it was a strange feeling. She sat thinking about what Martha had said. Suddenly she realized she could hear a noise. It was a strange sound, as if a child was crying. It was a long way away, but she was sure that it was inside the house. She turned round and looked at Martha.

'Can you hear someone crying?' she said.

Martha suddenly looked confused. 'It's just the wind,' she replied quickly. 'The wind makes such strange noises. Sometimes it sounds as if someone is lost on the moor.'

But Martha seemed worried about something. Mary stared at her. She was sure that the noise she had heard was not the wind. She did not believe that Martha was telling the truth.

It rained for the next few days, and Mary could not go outside. But one morning she woke and sat up in bed immediately.

'Look at the moor! Look at the moor!' she called to Martha.

The rain had stopped and the wind had blown the clouds away. There was a deep blue sky high above the moor. Mary had never seen such a blue sky.

'Yes,' said Martha cheerfully. 'The spring is coming.'

'I thought perhaps it always rained or looked dark in England,' Mary said.

'Oh no,' replied Martha. 'Yorkshire's the sunniest place on earth when it's sunny. Just wait till the gorse turns gold and the heather flowers. Then the heather looks like purple bells, and it's full of butterflies. You'll want to get out there first thing in the morning and stay out there all day, just like our Dickon!'

Martha went on cleaning out the fireplace. 'I'm going across the moor today,' she said. 'It's my day off and I'm going home to see my mother. Oh, I am glad!'

Mary had started to rather enjoy listening to Martha talk about her family. She especially liked to hear about Martha's mother and Dickon. When Martha told stories about what 'Mother' had done, they always sounded comfortable.

'I think I like your mother,' said Mary.

'Everyone likes my mother,' Martha replied. 'She's so sensible and hard-working, and friendly and clean.'

'I like Dickon too,' said Mary. 'And I've never seen him.'

'Well,' said Martha, 'I've told you that the birds and the sheep and ponies like him ... He's even got a little fox cub[43] that he keeps at home. And a crow[44] that flies about with him everywhere. Everyone likes Dickon, even the animals.'

After Martha had gone home, Mary felt lonelier than ever. She went out and ran round and round the fountain. And after that she felt a little better. Then she went into the kitchen garden and found Ben Weatherstaff working there. Even he seemed more cheerful on this beautiful morning.

'Springtime's coming,' he said. 'Things are beginning to happen in the flower gardens, down there in the dark. You'll see bits of green starting to stick out of the earth soon.'

'What will they be?' asked Mary.

'Crocuses[45] and snowdrops[45] and daffodils[45],' said Ben. 'You watch them. They'll grow a little bit more every day.'

At that moment, the robin flew down and hopped around near Mary's feet.

'Do you think he remembers me?' she asked Ben Weatherstaff.

'Of course he does!' he replied. 'He's never seen a little girl in the garden before, and he's trying to find out all about you.'

As Mary slowly walked away, she was thinking. She had begun to like the garden. And she had begun to like the robin, and Dickon, and Martha's mother. She was starting to like Martha, too. That felt like a lot of people for someone who had never really liked anyone before.

Mary went and walked in her favourite place, behind the long ivy-covered wall at the back of the kitchen gardens. And that was when the most interesting and exciting thing happened to her. She heard a twitter, looked down and saw the robin. He was hopping about on the earth. She knew that he had followed her, and she felt so pleased that she trembled[46] a little.

'You do remember me!' she cried. 'You do!'

The robin hopped among the bushes in the flower-bed. A dog had been digging a hole there, and the robin stopped to look for a worm in the earth. As Mary watched the robin, she noticed an old metal ring half-buried in the earth where the dog had been digging. When the robin flew up into a tree nearby, she reached down and picked the ring up. But it wasn't just a ring. It was an old key, and it looked as if it had been buried for a long time.

Mary stood up and looked at it. She felt almost frightened. 'Perhaps it has been buried for ten years,' she said in a whisper. 'Perhaps it is the key to the garden!' Suddenly she felt very excited. What would the garden look like now, after being shut up for so many years? If she could find the door, she could go into it every day. Nobody would know where she was. She liked that idea very much.

Mary put the key in her pocket and walked slowly up and down beside the wall. But the only thing she could see was thick ivy. She felt disappointed. But she decided to keep the key in her pocket. Then if she did find the hidden door, she would be ready.

4

Inside the Secret Garden

The next day, Martha was back at work. She was full of excitement about her visit home.

'When I'd helped Mother with all the baking and the washing I made the children a little cake,' she told Mary. 'And when they came in from playing on the moor, they just shouted for joy. And in the evening we all sat around the fire, and I told them all about you. They wanted to know all about the ship you sailed on from India! But Mother does worry about you all alone in a big place like this.'

Martha went on chattering about her day at home until she had finished tidying away Mary's breakfast things. Then she went back to the kitchen, and Mary put on her coat and hat and went outside into the gardens. She went to her special walk, and immediately noticed the robin hopping around at the bottom of the wall. When she saw him, she laughed.

'You showed me where the key was yesterday,' she said. 'You should really show me where the door is today. But I don't believe you know!'

The robin flew up onto the top of the wall and twittered loudly. What happened next really was very strange.

Mary had stepped forwards close to the robin, and at that moment a strong wind suddenly blew, lifting some of the ivy from the wall. Underneath, Mary saw a round knob[47] which had been covered by leaves. It was the knob of a door.

Mary put her hands under the leaves and began to pull and push them away. Her heart started beating hard, and her hands trembled a little with excitement. The robin kept singing and twittering, as if he was excited too. Mary could feel a metal hole.

It was the lock of the door which had been closed for ten years. Mary still had the key in her pocket, and she took it out and tried to put it in the hole. It fitted. Then she turned the key. It was difficult, and she had to use both hands. But the key turned.

Mary looked behind her, but there was no one coming. She took a deep breath and slowly pushed back the door. Then she went through the door and shut it behind her. She was breathing fast with excitement and delight.

She was standing inside the secret garden! It was a lovely, mysterious[48]-looking place. The high walls around it were covered with thick climbing roses. There were trees in the garden, and the climbing roses had run all over them. In places, the roses had grown from one tree to another and made lovely bridges. There were no leaves or roses on them now, just thin brown branches. But the way they hung from tree to tree looked so mysterious. It was different from any other place Mary had ever seen.

'How still it is!' Mary whispered to herself. Even the robin, who had flown to his treetop, was still. He sat watching her.

The garden was different from any other place Mary had ever seen.

Mary looked up at one of the mysterious curtains of roses.

'Are they all completely dead?' she wondered. 'I hope not.'

She did not want it to be a dead garden. If it were alive, how wonderful it would be.

As Mary walked around the garden, she felt as if she had found a world that was all her own. The robin flew down from his treetop and went from one bush to another. He twittered loudly, as if he were showing her things. In one of the corners of the garden, Mary could see that there had once been a flower bed. And sticking out of the earth there, she could see some green shoots[49]. She remembered what Ben Weatherstaff had said, and she bent down to look at them.

'Yes,' she whispered to herself. 'They are tiny growing things, and they might be crocuses or snowdrops or daffodils.'

All around the garden, Mary found lots more green shoots coming up out of the earth. She was feeling excited again.

'It isn't a dead garden,' she cried out softly to herself. 'Even if the roses are dead, there are other things that are alive.'

Mary did not know anything about gardening. But in some places the grass was very thick and the green shoots did not seem to have enough room to grow. Mary found a sharp piece of wood and dug away the weeds[50] and the grass.

'Now they look as if they can breathe,' said Mary, after she had finished the first ones. She enjoyed herself so much that she went on digging, all around the garden, making space around the green shoots. When it was time for lunch, she realized that she had been working for two or three hours. And she had felt happy all the time.

When Mary came in for lunch, Martha was delighted to see that she had bright red cheeks and bright eyes.

'Mother will be so pleased,' she said. 'She said you must stay outside as much as possible. And now look at the colour in your face!'

'I wish I had a little spade,' Mary said to Martha.

'What do you want a spade for?' asked Martha, laughing.

Mary thought for a moment. She had to be careful. If Mr Craven found out about the open door, he would probably get a new key and lock it up for ever. And that would be terrible.

'If I had a little spade,' Mary told her, 'I could do some digging like Ben Weatherstaff. Perhaps I could make a little garden and plant[51] some seeds[52] in it.'

'Well,' said Martha, thinking for a moment. 'I saw a nice little spade and fork in the shop in Thwaite last week. They sell flower seeds there too. Our Dickon often walks over to Thwaite. He knows all about planting seeds. Why don't we write him a letter? We can ask him to go and buy the spade and fork and some seeds at the same time.'

'Oh, yes, let's do that!' cried Mary, excited.

So that afternoon, Martha and Mary wrote a letter to Dickon. Mary had some money which Mrs Medlock had given her from Mr Craven. She put some of the money in the envelope with the letter, and gave it to Martha to send.

5

Dickon

The sun shone down for nearly a week on the secret garden. Mary loved the feeling that when she shut the door, no one knew where she was. Every day, she found more green shoots. They seemed to be coming up everywhere. Mary worked hard digging and pulling up weeds until the shoots had nice clear spaces around them. And the more she worked, the more she enjoyed herself.

During that week, Mary saw Ben Weatherstaff a lot.

He seemed happier to talk to her now. One day, when he seemed to be in a particularly good mood, Mary decided to ask him a question.

'If you wanted to make a flower garden,' she said, 'what would you plant?'

'Sweet-smelling things – but mostly roses,' Ben Weatherstaff replied.

'Do you like roses?' Mary asked.

Ben dug up a weed before he answered. 'Well, yes, I do,' he said. 'A young lady taught me about roses. She had a lot of them in a place she liked. And she loved them like children. But that was ten years ago now.'

'Where is she now?' asked Mary.

'She died,' Ben answered, digging his spade hard into the earth.

'What happened to the roses? Did they die too?' asked Mary, more interested than ever.

'Well, I liked them – and I liked her. So every year I used to go and work on them a bit, cutting them back and weeding around them. And some of them lived.'

'When they have no leaves and look grey and brown and dry, how can you tell whether they are dead or alive?' asked Mary.

'Look along the branches, and if you see some brown lumps[53],' Ben Weatherstaff replied. 'watch them after the rain.' Suddenly he stopped digging and looked curiously at Mary's excited face. 'Why do you care so much about roses all of a sudden?' he asked.

Mary felt her face grow red. She was almost afraid to answer.

'I – I want to say that – that I have a garden of my own,' she said. 'There is nothing for me to do. I – I have nothing – and no one.'

'Well,' said Ben Weatherstaff slowly. 'that's true.'

He said it in a strange way, and Mary thought he was perhaps feeling sorry for her. She had never felt sorry for herself. She had only felt tired and cross. But now the world seemed to be changing and getting nicer. She realized that she had found another person that she liked. She liked old Ben Weatherstaff, even though he was often so cross.

After Mary had finished talking to Ben, she walked down the long walk at the back of the secret garden. She decided to go up to the wood at the edge of the gardens, and look for rabbits. But as she got near to the wood, she heard a strange low whistling sound. Then she saw a very strange sight.

A boy was sitting under a tree, playing on a rough wooden pipe[54]. He was a funny-looking boy, and he was about twelve. His nose turned up, his cheeks were as red as poppies, and he had round, blue eyes. A brown squirrel[55] was watching him from a branch of the tree. And nearby two rabbits seemed to be listening to the noise of his pipe.

When the boy saw Mary, he held up his hand and spoke to her in a low voice.

'Don't move,' he said. 'It will frighten them away.'

Mary stood still. The boy stopped playing his pipe and began to get up very carefully. He moved so slowly, it was as if he wasn't moving at all. At last he stood up. The rabbits hopped away, and the squirrel ran back up the tree, but they didn't seem at all frightened.

'I'm Dickon,' the boy said. 'And I know you are Miss Mary. I've brought you a fork and a spade. They're really good ones! And I've got you some nice seeds, too.'

He had a wide, red mouth and his smile went right across his face. Mary knew nothing about boys, and she felt rather shy.

'Will you show the seeds to me?' she said.

When she came closer to him, she noticed that he had a clean fresh smell of heather, grass and leaves. It was a nice smell. And when she looked into his funny face with the red cheeks and the blue eyes, she forgot that she was feeling shy.

Dickon took out some small paper bags.

'There are lots of poppies, look,' he said. 'They'll grow wherever you throw the seeds.'

He stopped and turned his head quickly.

'There's a robin calling us,' he said. And sure enough they heard a loud twitter from the bushes. Dickon turned towards Mary. 'Does he know you?' he asked.

'He knows me a little,' said Mary. 'Is he really calling us?'

'Oh, yes,' laughed Dickon. He moved closer to the bushes, and made a sound almost like the robin's own twitter. The robin twittered back as if it were answering a question.

'Oh yes, he's a friend of yours,' said Dickon. 'I can see that!'

'Do you understand everything birds say?' said Mary.

'I think I do, and they think I do,' Dickon smiled. 'Sometimes I think perhaps I am a bird, or a fox or a rabbit!'

He laughed, and started telling Mary about the seeds once more. 'Why don't I come and plant them for you?' he said. 'Where's your garden?'

Mary said nothing. Her face turned red and then pale.

'Didn't they give you a bit of garden?' said Dickon.

Mary looked at him.

'I don't know anything about boys,' she said slowly. 'Could you keep a secret, if I told you one? It's a big secret. I think if anyone found out, I would die!'

'I'm keeping secrets all the time,' said Dickon. 'If I told all the other boys about birds' nests[56] and foxes' cubs and things, nothing on the moor would be safe.'

Mary said nothing for a moment. Then she made up her mind.

'I've stolen a garden,' she said, very fast. 'Nobody wants it. Perhaps everything in it is dead already. I don't know. But they can't take it away from me! They can't!' She felt hot and cross again.

'Where is it?' asked Dickon gently.

'Come with me and I'll show you,' Mary said, getting up. And she led Dickon to the ivy-covered wall and took him through the door into the secret garden.

'Here it is,' she said. 'It's a secret garden. And I'm the only one in the world who wants it to be alive.'

Dickon looked all around. He breathed out in surprise.

'Well,' he almost whispered. 'What a strange and pretty place. It's like walking into a dream.'

For two or three minutes, he stood looking around him while Mary watched him. Then he began to walk softly around.

'I never thought I'd see this place,' he whispered at last. 'Martha told me there was a garden that no one went into. We used to wonder what it was like.'

'Will there be roses?' Mary whispered. 'I thought perhaps they were all dead.'

'No, not all of them,' Dickon answered. 'Look here!'

He walked over to one of the branches and took out his knife. There were lots of shoots on the branch, and most of them were hard, dry-grey. But one was brownish-green.

'This here is a new bit,' said Dickon, pointing at it. 'It's as alive as you or me.'

'Oh, I am glad!' cried Mary.

They went from tree to tree and from bush to bush. Dickon was very strong and clever with his knife. He knew how to cut the dead wood away. And he knew when a branch still had green life in it. He showed Mary how to use the fork, and they went around the garden digging and pulling out weeds.

'There's a lot of work to do here!' said Dickon, looking around happily.

'Will you come again and help me do it?' Mary said. 'Oh, do come, Dickon!'

'I'll come every day if you want me to,' he answered. 'But I don't want it to look like a gardener's garden. It's nice like this, with the roses all running wild. I wouldn't like it all neat and tidy, would you?'

'Let's not make it tidy,' said Mary. 'It wouldn't be a secret garden if it was tidy.'

Dickon stood rubbing his head for a moment.

'It *is* a secret garden,' he said, 'but someone else must have been in here since it was shut up ten years ago.'

'But the door was locked and the key was buried,' said Mary. 'No one could get in.'

'That's true,' said Dickon. 'But I think someone's cut back these roses a bit in the last ten years.' As he started digging again, he leant forward to smell the freshly-turned earth. 'Oh, when there are things growing, and birds singing and whistling, it makes me feel good.'

They worked harder and more happily than ever. Mary was sorry when she realized it was dinner time.

'I shall have to go,' she said sadly. She didn't want to leave Dickon. It all seemed too much like a dream. She couldn't believe that he would really be there when she came back.

'You – you would never tell?' she asked Dickon.

'Imagine you were a thrush[57] and you showed me your nest. Do you think I'd tell anyone?' Dickon smiled. 'Not me. You're as safe as a thrush.'

When she got inside, Mary told Martha all about meeting Dickon. But she was very careful. She didn't say anything about the secret garden. Then she ate her dinner as quickly as possible. She was getting ready to go outside again when Martha stopped her.

'I've got something to tell you,' Martha said. 'Mr Craven came back this morning and he wants to see you.'

Mary turned pale.

'Why? Why does he want to see me?' she asked.

'Mrs Medlock says that my mother saw him in the village yesterday,' said Martha. 'And she said something to him but I don't know what she said. He's going away again tomorrow. He probably won't come back again until the autumn or winter. And he wants to see you before he goes. Mrs Medlock is going to come and get you in a minute.'

Mr Craven was sitting in a chair in front of the fire. He was not really a hunchback, but he had high, slightly crooked shoulders. His black hair was white in places.

'This is Miss Mary, sir,' said Mrs Medlock.

'You can leave her here,' said Mr Craven, and he looked over his shoulder at Mary. 'Come here!' he said, as Mrs Medlock left the room.

He was not ugly. But his face was miserable[58], and he looked worried.

'Are you well?' he asked Mary. 'You are very thin.'

'I am getting fatter,' said Mary, in her stiff little voice.

'I forgot you,' he said. 'I should have got you a teacher, but I forgot.'

What an unhappy face he had! His black eyes hardly seemed to see Mary. It was as if they were seeing something else.

'Please,' said Mary. 'Please don't make me have a teacher yet.'

'That's what Mrs Sowerby said,' said Mr Craven. 'Martha's mother. I met her yesterday, and she was worried about you. She said you should play outside. She thought you should get stronger before you have a teacher.'

'I want to play outside,' Mary answered. She tried to stop her voice trembling. 'It makes me feel strong when I play in the wind from the moor.'

Mr Craven was watching her.

'Where do you play?' he asked.

'Everywhere,' said Mary quietly. 'I run around, and look for things growing up out of the earth. I don't do anything wrong.'

'Don't look so frightened,' said Mr Craven in a worried voice. 'You may do what you like. I am not good at looking after children. I am too ill and I have too many things to think about. But I want you to be happy and comfortable. Play outside as much as you like. You can go anywhere you like. Is there anything you want?' he added suddenly. 'Do you want toys, books, dolls?'

'Could I ...' said Mary, her voice trembling, 'Could I have a bit of earth?'

Mr Craven looked surprised.

'Earth?' he said. 'What do you mean?'

'I want to plant some seeds and watch them grow,' said Mary.

Mr Craven stared at her and put his hands over his face for a moment. Then he got up and walked slowly across the room. When he spoke to her again his eyes were soft and kind.

'You can have as much earth as you want,' he said. 'You remind me of someone else who loved the earth and things that grow. When you see a bit of earth you want, take it, child. Make it come alive. Now, you must go. I am tired.' He touched the bell to call Mrs Medlock. 'Goodbye. I shall be away all summer.'

When Mrs Medlock had led Mary back to her own corridor, she ran into her room. Martha was waiting there for her.

'I can have a garden!' Mary cried, excited. 'And I am not going to have a teacher until I am stronger! Mr Craven said that I can do what I like.'

Mary ran as quickly as she could out to the garden. She knew that she had been away for a long time. When she went under the ivy and through the door, she saw that Dickon was not there. The garden fork and spade were lying under a tree, but the secret garden was empty.

'He's gone,' said Mary sadly. 'Oh, was it all just a dream?'

Then she saw a piece of paper lying by the fork and spade. There was a picture on the paper, and some writing. She couldn't see what the picture was at first, but then she realized. It was a bird sitting on a nest. Underneath, the writing said, 'I will come back.'

6

A Meeting in the Night

Mary took the picture back to the house and showed it to Martha.

'Oh, our Dickon's clever,' she said proudly. 'That's a picture of a thrush on her nest. It almost looks real.'

Suddenly Mary understood. The picture was like a message. Dickon wanted to show her that he would keep her secret.

Mary hoped that he would come back the next day. She fell asleep feeling excited about the morning. But in the night she was woken by the sound of heavy rain. It was beating against her window, and the wind was whistling around the house. Mary felt miserable and angry. Now she wouldn't be able to go to the garden in the morning.

She could not go to sleep again. After she had been lying awake for about an hour, she suddenly sat up in bed. She had heard something.

'That's not the noise of the wind,' she said in a loud whisper. 'It's that crying I heard before, when I first arrived here.'

She listened for a few minutes, and she became more and more sure. She got out of bed and stood up.

'I am going to find out what it is,' she said.

She followed the noise of the crying along the corridors, her heart beating loudly. At last she came to a door with a light coming from underneath. The crying was coming from inside.

Mary pushed the door open and stepped inside a large room. There was lots of beautiful old furniture in the room. A fire was burning gently. There was also a big bed. And on the bed a boy was lying, crying miserably.

The boy had a sharp white face with big grey eyes and lots of hair. He looked up at Mary and his eyes opened wide.

'Who are you?' he said in a half-frightened whisper. 'Are you a ghost?'

'No, I'm not,' answered Mary. 'Are you?'

'No,' the boy replied after a moment or so. Mary thought that he looked ill. 'I am Colin. Colin Craven. Who are you?'

'I am Mary Lennox. Mr Craven is my uncle.'

'He is my father,' said the boy.

'Your father!' gasped[59] Mary. 'No one ever told me he had a boy!'

'Come here,' said Colin, watching her carefully with a worried face.

Mary came close to the bed. The boy put out his hand and touched her arm.

'Where did you come from?' he asked.

'From my room,' said Mary. 'I heard someone crying. I wanted to see who it was. Why were you crying?'

'Because I couldn't go to sleep,' said Colin. 'Tell me your name again.'

'Mary Lennox. Did no one tell you that I live here now?'

'No,' the boy answered. 'They were probably afraid to tell me. I don't let people see me or talk about me.'

'Why?' asked Mary.

On the bed a boy was lying, crying miserably.

'Because I'm always ill. I'm always having to lie down. My father won't let people talk about me either. If I live, I may be a hunchback, but I shan't live.'

'Oh, what a strange house this is!' said Mary. 'Everything is secret. Rooms are locked up and gardens are locked up. What about you? Have you been locked up too?'

'No,' replied Colin. 'I stay here because I don't want to go out. I get too tired.'

'If you don't like people to see you,' she said, 'do you want me to go away?'

'No,' he said. 'I want to hear about you.'

Mary sat down near the bed. She wanted to stay in this hidden room. She wanted to talk to this mysterious boy.

'What do you want me to tell you?' she asked.

Colin wanted to know how long she had been at Misselthwaite. He asked where her room was and what she did during the day. He made her tell him all about India and her journey back to England. Mary found out lots of things about Colin, too. He had lots of wonderful toys and things. Whenever he asked for things, people always brought them to him. And if he didn't want to do something, no one made him do it.

'Everyone has to please me,' Colin told her. 'I get ill when I am angry. No one believes I shall live long enough to grow up.'

'Does your father come and see you?' Mary asked.

'Sometimes,' Colin answered, and his face suddenly looked dark and angry. 'But he doesn't want to see me. My mother died when I was born. It makes my father feel miserable when he looks at me. He almost hates me.'

'He hates the garden because she died,' Mary said, almost to herself. 'That was why he locked the garden door and buried the key.'

Colin sat up a little, and turned towards Mary.

'What garden door did he lock?' he asked. He was suddenly interested.

'It – it was a garden your mother used to like,' said Mary nervously. 'He locked the door ten years ago. No one – no one knows where he buried the key.'

'What sort of garden is it?' asked Colin, excited.

'No one has been into it for ten years,' said Mary carefully.

But it was too late to be careful. Colin was too much like Mary. He, too, was excited about the idea of a hidden garden. He asked her lots of questions. Where was the garden? Had Mary ever looked for the door? Had she ever asked the gardeners?

'The gardeners won't talk about it,' said Mary. 'I think your father told them not to say anything.'

'I shall make them tell me,' said Colin.

'Could you do that?' asked Mary, starting to feel worried.

'Everyone has to please me,' said Colin. 'If I live, this house will be mine one day.'

'Do you really think you won't live?' Mary asked. She wanted him to forget about the garden.

'Everyone says that I won't,' replied Colin. 'They think I don't know. At first they thought that I was too little to understand. And now they think that I don't hear. But I do. My doctor is my father's cousin. He is quite poor. If I die, he will have Misselthwaite when my father dies. So I don't think he wants me to live.'

'Do you want to live?' asked Mary.

'No,' Colin said, sounding cross and tired. 'My father is afraid that I will be a hunchback like him. I don't want to die, though. When I feel ill I lie here and think about dying. And then I cry and cry. But let's not talk about that. Let's talk about the garden. Don't you want to see it?'

'Yes,' Mary said quietly.

'I do,' Colin went on. 'I don't think I ever wanted to see anything before. But I want to see that garden. I want to find the key and unlock the door. They could take me there in my wheelchair[60]. I am going to make them open the door. They have to please me. I will make them take me there. And I will let you go too.'

He had become quite excited, and his large eyes were shining.

Mary's heart was beating hard. Everything would be spoiled. Dickon would never come back. She would never again feel like a thrush with a safely hidden nest.

'Oh, don't! Don't do that!' she cried out.

He stared at her.

'Why not?' he asked, surprised. 'You said you wanted to see it.'

'I do,' she answered, feeling as if she might cry. 'But if you make them open the door like that, it will never be a secret again.' She took a deep breath. 'You see, if we are the only people who know, perhaps we can find the door. Perhaps we can go in and shut it behind us. And then no one would know that we were inside. Oh, don't you see? It would be so much nicer if it was a secret.'

'I've never had a proper secret,' said Colin.

'Don't make them take you to the garden,' said Mary. 'I'm sure I can find out how to get into it. And then perhaps we could find a boy who could push your wheelchair. We could go alone. Then it would always be a secret garden.'

'I should like that,' Colin said slowly. His eyes looked dreamy.

'I have been here a long time,' said Mary. 'Shall I go away now? You look sleepy.'

'I am. But I am glad you came,' said Colin.

'So am I,' said Mary. 'I shall come as often as I can. But I will have to look every day for the garden door.'

'Yes, you must,' said Colin. 'And you can tell me about it afterwards. Do you know Martha?'

'Yes, I know her very well,' said Mary, surprised. 'She brings me my meals.'

'She looks after me when my nurse isn't here,' said Colin. 'Martha will tell you when to come.'

So Martha already knew about Colin! That was why she looked so worried when Mary asked her about the crying. Suddenly Mary understood.

'I wish I could go to sleep before you leave me,' Colin said a little shyly.

'Shut your eyes,' said Mary, moving closer to the bed. 'I shall hold your hand and sing to you quietly. My servants used to do that for me in India.'

'I would like that,' said Colin sleepily.

It was strange, but Mary felt sorry for Colin. She didn't want him to lie there awake. So she sat close to the bed and held his hand. And she sang quietly to him until his eyes shut and he was asleep. Then she got up quietly and went back to her room.

7

Colin

It was still raining in the morning, and Mary couldn't go outside. She didn't see Martha until the afternoon. But when Martha came to bring her her tea, Mary told her the news at once.

'I have found out what the crying was,' Mary said. 'I heard it in the night and I wanted to see where it was coming from. So I went to look, and I found Colin.'

'Oh, Miss Mary,' cried Martha. 'You shouldn't have done that! They will be cross with me. They will send me away!'

'They won't send you away,' said Mary. 'Colin was pleased that I came. We talked and talked. He asked me all about India.'

Martha gasped in amazement.

'I don't believe you!' she said. 'Colin won't let people look at him. When they do, he has one of his tantrums[61]. He screams and cries so much it frightens us all. Was he *really* nice to you?'

'I think he almost liked me,' Mary said. 'What's the matter with him?'

'Nobody really knows,' said Martha. 'Mr Craven nearly went mad when he was born, because Mrs Craven had died. He wouldn't look at the baby. He said that Colin would just be another hunchback. Everyone worries that his back is weak. So they make him lie down and they don't let him walk. Dr Craven made him wear a metal thing on his back once. But another doctor came from London and told him to take it off. He was very angry. He said that Colin takes too much medicine[62]. He said people shouldn't let him do what he wants all the time.'

'Do you think he will die?' asked Mary.

'Mother says it's difficult to live when you're like that. He doesn't get any fresh air. He lies on his back all day taking medicine and reading books.'

A bell rang, and Martha got up to go. When she came back, she looked surprised.

'Well, you have put him in a good mood[63],' she said. 'He's sitting up on his sofa reading. He wants you to go and see him.'

Mary was pleased. She wanted to see Colin very much. Not as much as she wanted to see Dickon. But she did want to see him.

Colin's room looked even more beautiful in daylight. There were colourful rugs and pictures, and lots of books. Colin was sitting on the sofa wearing a dressing gown[64].

'Come in,' he said. 'I've been thinking about you all morning.'

'I've been thinking about you, too,' answered Mary. 'You know, Martha is very frightened. She thinks that Mrs Medlock will send her away. She says Mrs Medlock will think Martha told me about you.'

Colin frowned.

'Go and tell Martha to come here,' he said. 'She is in the next room.'

Mary went and brought her back. Poor Martha was trembling.

'You know that you have to do what I tell you,' Colin said to her in a hard voice.

'Yes, sir,' said Martha, turning red.

'Medlock has to do what I tell her too. So when I ask you to bring Mary here, you must bring her. And if Medlock says anything about it, I'll send *her* away,' he said importantly. 'Now go.'

When Martha had gone, Colin saw that Mary was staring at him.

'Why are you looking at me like that?' he asked. 'What were you thinking?'

'I was thinking that I saw a prince in India once,' Mary replied. 'He spoke to his people just like you spoke to Martha. Everybody had to do what he said. And I was also thinking how different you are from Dickon.'

'Who is Dickon?' Colin said.

'He is Martha's brother,' said Mary. 'He is not like anyone else in the world. He plays on his pipe and the foxes and squirrels and birds come and listen to him. He knows about everything that grows or lives on the moor. He knows all about eggs and nests. And he knows where all the animals live. But he keeps it a secret. He doesn't want other boys to frighten them.'

Colin lay back on the sofa and his eyes grew larger.

'Tell me some more about him,' he said.

So Mary told Colin about the moor, and about Dickon's cottage and the fourteen people who lived there. She talked about Dickon's mother. And she talked about the green shoots that were sticking up out of the black earth.

'You never see anything if you are ill,' said Colin quietly.

'You can't if you stay in a room,' said Mary.

'I couldn't go on the moor,' said Colin. 'How could I? I am going to die.'

Mary didn't like the way Colin talked about dying. He almost sounded proud of it.

'Let's not talk about dying,' she said. 'Let's talk about living. Dickon is always talking about living things. He's always looking up in the sky to watch birds flying. Or looking down at the earth to watch things growing. Let's talk about Dickon.'

It was the best thing she could have said. Mary talked more than she had ever talked before. And Colin talked and listened more than he had ever done. They both began to laugh about nothing. And suddenly they seemed just like normal healthy happy children. They no longer seemed like a hard unloving little girl and a poor crooked boy who thought he was going to die.

It rained for the rest of that week, so Mary couldn't go to the secret garden or see Dickon. But she enjoyed herself very much. Every day, she spent hours with Colin in his room. They talked about gardens or Dickon or the cottage on the moor, and they looked at Colin's books.

Mrs Medlock had been shocked the first time she walked into Master Colin's room and found Mary there. But Colin told her that Mary made him feel better. He said that he wanted her to come and talk to him whenever he asked.

Mary was very careful about the secret garden when she talked to Colin. She still wasn't sure whether he would be able to keep the secret. But she thought perhaps if Colin met Dickon and saw things growing, he wouldn't think about dying so much. She knew that the gardens and the fresh air had been good for her. She had grown stronger and fatter, and her cheeks were red. Perhaps the fresh air would be good for Colin too.

8

A Tantrum

On the first morning when the sky was blue again, Mary woke very early. The sun was pouring in through the windows. She jumped out of bed and ran to open the window. The moor was blue, and the fresh air that blew in was warm.

'I can't wait!' Mary said, excited. 'I'm going to see the garden!'

She knew how to dress herself by now. She put on her clothes and ran downstairs. No one was awake because it was so early, but she unlocked a small side door. And then she stepped outside. The sky was so blue and full of spring-time light that she wanted to sing. She ran towards the secret garden. In all the flower beds, things had started to grow. Mary could even see purple and yellow crocuses starting to come out. The world was waking up.

When Mary arrived at the door of the secret garden, she heard a strange low sound. Looking up, she saw a crow landing on top of the wall. He made her a little nervous, and she felt glad when he flew away across the garden. But when she went into the garden, she saw that he had landed on an apple tree. Under the apple tree was a little fox cub. Both animals were watching Dickon, who was working hard on the grass below.

Mary ran across the grass to him.

'Oh, Dickon! Dickon!' she cried out. 'How did you get here so early?'

'I couldn't stay in bed!' he laughed. 'The world's begun again this morning. And the garden was lying here waiting. I ran like mad all the way here, shouting and singing! And these two came with me!'

As he spoke, the little fox cub got up and moved next to him. And the crow flew down and sat quietly on his shoulder.

'Oh, Dickon!' said Mary. 'I'm so happy!'

There was so much to see. There were leaf-buds[65] growing on the rose branches. And there were thousands of new green shoots pushing up through the earth. There was every joy on earth in the secret garden that morning. Even the robin had a special surprise for them. They suddenly saw him flying through the trees with something in his beak[66]. Dickon stood quite still and put his hand on Mary's arm.

'He's found a mate[67] and he's building his nest,' he whispered to her. 'That's part of spring-time. We mustn't frighten him.'

'There's something I want to tell you,' whispered Mary. 'Do you know about Colin?'

Dickon turned his head to look at her in surprise.

'What do you know about him?' he asked.

Mary told Dickon about finding Colin in his room.

'Colin is afraid of becoming a hunchback like his father,' said Mary. 'He's so afraid of it that he won't sit up.'

Dickon thought for a few minutes.

'I knew there was a little boy who was ill', he said. 'And I knew that Mr Craven didn't like people talking about him. If he was out here, he wouldn't think about being a hunchback. Do you think we could get him to come out here?'

'I've been wondering that myself,' said Mary.

'It'd be good for him, I'm sure,' said Dickon. 'I could push his wheelchair. I'm sure we could get him out here.'

They were so busy in the garden that Mary didn't go and see Colin all day. When she finally said goodbye to Dickon and came into the house for tea, she was excited about seeing Colin. She wanted to tell him about Dickon's fox cub and the crow.

But when she went to her room, Martha was waiting there, looking worried.

'Oh, I wish you'd gone to see him today,' Martha said. 'He's been getting close to a tantrum all afternoon.'

When Mary went into Colin's room, he was lying on his back in his bed. His nurse was sitting in the corner of the room. Colin did not turn his head towards Mary when she came in.

'Why didn't you get up?' Mary asked him.

'I did get up this morning,' Colin answered, without looking at her. 'But you didn't come. So I told them to put me back in bed this afternoon. Where have you been?'

'I was working in the garden with Dickon,' said Mary.

Colin frowned and looked at her.

'I won't let that boy come here if you stay with him all the time,' he said.

Mary grew silently angry.

'If you send Dickon away, I'll never come into this room again,' she said.

'I'll make you!' said Colin. 'You're so selfish!'

'You're more selfish than I am,' said Mary. 'You're the most selfish boy I ever saw.'

'I'm not!' snapped Colin. 'I'm not selfish, because I'm always ill,' he said. 'And anyway, I'm going to die.'

'You're not!' snapped Mary. 'You just say that. I think you're proud of it!'

Colin's face had gone white and red, and he was shaking.

'I felt a lump in my back,' he choked[68]. 'I felt it. I am going to turn into a hunchback, and then I shall die.'

'You didn't feel a lump,' said Mary, still angry. 'There's nothing wrong with your stupid back. Turn over and let me look at it. Nurse! Come here and show me his back!'

The nurse came up to the bed, looking a little frightened.

'Show her!' Colin cried. 'Then she'll see!'

The nurse helped Colin turn over, and Mary looked up and down his poor thin back.

'There's nothing there!' she said at last. 'There are no lumps. If you ever say there's a lump again, I shall laugh!'

For years, Colin had lain in his bed thinking that he was ill. Everyone had been frightened of him. So no one had ever told him that there was nothing wrong with him. But now, hearing this angry little girl, he actually felt that she might be telling the truth.

'I didn't know that he thought he had a lump on his back,' said the nurse quietly. 'There's no lump. His back is weak because he doesn't sit up.'

Colin turned to look at her. Big tears were running down his face.

'Do you think – do you think I will live long enough to grow up?' he asked.

'You probably will if you get lots of fresh air,' said the nurse.

'I'll look after him,' Mary said to the nurse. 'You can go if you like.'

As soon as the nurse had gone, Colin pulled Mary's hand.

'Tell me, Mary.' he said. 'Have you – have you found the way into the secret garden yet?'

Mary looked at Colin's poor little tired face and her heart softened.

'I think I may have found the way,' she answered. 'And if you promise not to have any more tantrums, I will tell you about it tomorrow.'

Colin's hand trembled.

'Oh, Mary!' he said. 'If I could go into the garden, I think I would live long enough to grow up!'

'Lie quietly,' Mary said. 'And I shall tell you what I think the garden might look like.'

And quietly, Mary began to talk about the secret garden. She talked about roses that might have climbed all over the trees and the walls. She talked about crocuses that might be turning purple and yellow. And she talked about a robin that might be building its nest. And when she looked up, Colin had fallen asleep.

9

'The Spring has Come!'

The next morning, Mary woke late. When she got up, she saw that there was a wooden box on her table.

'Mr Craven sent it to you,' said Martha, excited.

Mary opened the box. There were several beautiful books. Two of them were about gardens. There were also two or three games, and a beautiful little writing case. Mary had not expected Mr Craven to remember her and her hard little heart grew quite warm. She ate her breakfast quickly, and went straight to Colin's room, carrying the box. He was lying on his bed looking pale and tired, but he was pleased to see her. Mary showed him the presents, and together they looked at the garden books.

'Mary,' he said after a while, 'I wish I hadn't said those things about sending Dickon away yesterday.' Mary could see that Colin was thinking. 'You know,' he went on, 'I wouldn't mind if Dickon saw me. I want to meet him.'

'I'm glad you said that,' answered Mary, 'because Dickon would like to come and see you too. I could ask him to come tomorrow, if you like.'

'Oh! Oh!' Colin cried out, excited.

'And there's something else, too,' said Mary. 'Can you promise to keep a secret?' she said. 'Can you really promise?'

Mary's face was so serious that Colin almost whispered his answer.

'Yes – yes!'

'There is a door into the garden,' said Mary. 'I found it. It is under the ivy on the wall.'

Colin's eyes grew bigger and bigger. He almost couldn't breathe. Then he took hold of her hands and pulled her towards him.

'Oh, Mary!' he cried out. 'Will I be able to see it? Will I be able to go into it? Will I live long enough?'

'Of course you will!' she said a little crossly. 'Don't be silly!'

And because she spoke so sensibly, he started to laugh at himself. Mary sat down next to his bed. After a few moments, she told him all about the secret garden. And this time, she did not tell him what she thought it would be like. She told him how it really was. He listened full of excitement and delight.

'It's just how you thought it would be!' he said at last.

Mary thought for a couple of minutes. And then she told Colin the truth.

'I had already seen it – and I had been in it,' she said. 'I found the key and got in weeks ago. But I didn't tell you because I wasn't sure that you could keep a secret.'

The next morning, Mary and Colin ate their breakfast together with the morning air pouring in through the window. Colin ate a good breakfast, and Mary watched him with interest.

'You will start to get fatter, just like me,' she said.

'I felt hungry this morning,' said Colin. 'Perhaps it's the fresh air coming from the window. When do you think Dickon will come?'

They didn't have to wait long. A few minutes later, the door opened and Martha came in.

'Excuse me, sir,' she said. 'Here's Dickon and his animals.'

Dickon came in smiling his nicest wide smile. He was holding a newborn lamb[69] in his arms, and the little fox cub was walking next to him. Two squirrels were looking out of his pockets, and the crow sat on his shoulder.

Colin slowly sat up and stared and stared. He had never talked to another boy before. He was so curious and so excited that he forgot to speak.

But Dickon was not at all shy. He walked over to Colin's sofa, and put the lamb quietly onto Colin's knees. It immediately started rubbing its nose against Colin's dressing gown.

'What is it doing?' asked Colin. 'What does it want?'

'It's hungry,' said Dickon, smiling. He took a feeding bottle of milk out of his pocket and put it in the lamb's mouth. And the children watched as the lamb drank the milk all down quickly and then fell asleep on Colin's knee.

After that, the children wanted to know all about the lamb. Dickon told them that he had found it on the moor three days before. Its mother had died, and it was hungry. So he had wrapped it up in his coat, and carried it home.

'It was half dead with cold when I found it,' said Dickon. 'But I fed it some warm milk, and it lay down next to the fire, and soon started to look better.'

While Dickon talked, the squirrels ran up and down the big trees outside Colin's room. And the crow flew in and out of the open window. After Colin had asked Dickon endless questions about the animals, the children looked at the pictures in Mary's garden books. They also talked about the flowers that were growing in the secret garden.

'I'm going to see them!' cried Colin. 'I'm going to see them!'

'Yes, you are,' said Mary. 'And you're going to see them soon!'

10

Colin Goes into the Secret Garden

But the children had to wait for more than a week. The next few days were very windy, and then Colin got a cold. Normally, when things did not happen the way he wanted, Colin had big tantrums. But the children were so busy planning his visit to the secret garden that Colin did not have time to get upset.

At last the day they had been waiting for came. Colin sent for Mrs Medlock in the morning.

'I am going out in my wheelchair this afternoon,' he said. 'If I like the fresh air, I may go out every day. When I go, all the gardeners must stay away from the kitchen gardens. I will go out at about two o'clock. I will tell them when they can go back to their work.'

Mrs Medlock had almost gasped in surprise when Colin started talking. He had always said that fresh air would give him a cold and kill him.

'Things are changing in this house,' Mrs Medlock said to the nurse after she had left Colin's room. 'That girl from India has done something to Master Colin. I don't know what it is. But there's something different about him.'

After lunch, the nurse helped Colin to get dressed, and a servant carried him downstairs to his wheelchair while Mary walked behind. Dickon was waiting outside. The nurse and the servant arranged Colin's rugs and cushions, and then they went back inside.

When they had gone, Dickon began to push the wheelchair slowly and carefully. Mary walked next to it, and Colin lay back and looked up at the sky. The small snowy clouds were like white birds floating above the blue. The wind blew softly down from the moor, bringing a sweet clear smell.

'What's that smell?' Colin asked.

'It's the gorse on the moor opening out,' answered Dickon. 'The bees will be busy today!'

The gardeners had all gone, as Colin had asked. But when the children arrived at the long walk, they started to whisper.

'This is where I used to walk,' said Mary quietly. 'And this is where the robin showed me the key.'

Colin's eyes grew bigger and bigger.

'And this,' said Mary, stepping onto the flower bed and lifting up the ivy, 'this is the door!'

Colin gasped as Mary turned the handle and opened the door. Then Dickon pushed the wheelchair through the door and into the garden. Colin covered his eyes with his hands until the wheelchair had stopped. Only then did he take them away and look round and round. Everywhere there were little patches[70] of gold and purple and white. Little green leaves were growing on the branches and the walls. And all around them they heard birds fluttering[71] their wings.

The sun fell on Colin's face like a hand with a lovely touch. And Mary and Dickon stood and stared at him in surprise. He looked so strange and different. A little bit of colour had touched his face and neck and hands.

'I shall get well!' he cried out. 'Mary! Dickon! I shall get well! And I shall live for ever and ever!'

Dickon and Mary pushed the wheelchair slowly round and round the garden, stopping all the time to show Colin things. They showed him buds that were opening and leaves that were just coming out. They showed him crocuses coming up from the earth. There were so many new things to look at that afternoon. Every hour the sunshine seemed to get more golden.

After a while, Dickon and Mary pulled Colin's wheelchair under the plum tree, which was covered in snow-white blossom[72]. They did a little bit of work in the garden, and Colin watched them.

'Look!' cried Dickon suddenly, pointing across the garden at a flash[73] of red. 'There's the robin! He's been looking for food for his mate.'

Colin looked up and saw the robin flying into the trees with a worm in his beak. Then the boy sat back in his chair, laughing a little with happiness.

'I don't want this afternoon to end,' he said. 'But I shall come back tomorrow, and the next day, and the next day. I'm going to see everything grow here. And I'm going to grow here myself.'

'You will,' said Dickon. 'Soon you'll be walking about and digging here like us.'

Colin's face went red.

'Walk!' he said. 'Dig! Shall I?'

Mary and Dickon looked at each other. They had never asked Colin why he did not walk. They did not know if there was anything wrong with his legs.

'Of course you will,' said Dickon after a moment. 'You've got legs, just like us, haven't you?'

'There's nothing wrong with them,' Colin answered. 'But they are so thin and weak. I'm afraid to stand up because they shake so much.'

'When you stop being afraid, you'll stand on them,' Dickon said.

They were all quiet for a little while. The sun was dropping lower in the sky. Even the animals had stopped moving about. Dickon and Mary were both surprised when Colin suddenly said in a frightened whisper:

'Who is that man?'

Dickon and Mary jumped up. Colin was pointing at the high wall.

'Look!' he whispered excitedly. 'Look!'

Mary and Dickon looked up. Ben Weatherstaff was standing at the top of a ladder[74], looking crossly over the wall at them. Mary walked towards him.

'I always thought you were a bad one,' he said to her, shaking his fist[75]. 'Always asking questions. How on earth did you get in here?'

Suddenly, Ben Weatherstaff stopped shaking his fist and his mouth dropped open. Dickon was pushing Colin's wheelchair across the grass towards Mary. Ben stared at Colin. He looked as if he was seeing a ghost.

'Do you know who I am?' Colin said importantly.

Ben Weatherstaff rubbed his hand over his eyes.

'Yes, I do,' he said. 'I can see your mother's eyes staring at me out of that face. I don't know how you got here. But you are that poor boy who can't walk.'

Colin went bright red and sat up.

'I can walk!' he shouted. 'I can!'

'You – you haven't got a crooked back?' asked Ben.

'No!' shouted Colin.

'And you haven't got crooked legs?' Ben said in a shaky voice.

It was too much for Colin. Suddenly his anger made him stronger than he had ever been before.

'Come here!' he shouted to Dickon, pulling the rugs[76] off his wheelchair. 'Come here now!'

Dickon rushed to Colin's side. Mary felt herself turn pale.

'He can do it! He can do it!' she whispered to herself.

Dickon threw the rugs on the ground and took Colin's arm. His thin legs came out and his feet were on the grass. Then Colin was standing up, looking strangely tall. He threw his head back and his eyes shone.

Then Colin was standing up, looking strangely tall.

'Look at me!' he shouted up at Ben Weatherstaff. 'Just look at me!'

'He's as straight as I am,' cried Dickon.

Then Ben Weatherstaff did something very strange. He choked and put his hands together, and tears ran down his cheeks.

'Oh, it was all lies!' he said. 'You're as thin as a stick and as white as a sheet. But you're not crooked. You'll be a fine man one day. God bless you.'

Dickon held Colin's arms strongly, but Colin stood straighter and straighter.

'I'm your master when my father is away,' Colin said to Ben. 'You must do what I say. This is my garden. You mustn't say anything about it. Now get down from that ladder. Go out to the long walk and Mary will meet you there. She'll bring you here. I want to talk to you. We did not want you, but now you will have to be in the secret.'

Ben Weatherstaff still couldn't stop looking at Colin's face.

'Oh, my boy,' he almost whispered. Then he added, 'Yes, sir, yes, sir.' And his head disappeared as he went down the ladder.

Mary ran across the grass to meet him, and Colin turned to Dickon. His cheeks were red.

'I'm going to walk to that tree,' Colin said, pointing at a tree close by.

He walked to the tree. Dickon held his arm, but he walked without stopping. When Ben Weatherstaff came through the door, he saw Colin standing there.

'Look at me!' said Colin. 'Am I a hunchback? Have I got crooked legs?

'No,' said Ben, looking him up and down. 'You haven't. Why don't you sit down, young master. And tell me what to do.'

Dickon had put a rug under the tree, and Colin sat down on it.

'What work do you do in the gardens, Weatherstaff?' he asked.

'Anything they tell me to,' Ben answered. 'They kept me here because your mother liked me.'

'My mother?' said Colin, and he looked about quietly. 'This was her garden, wasn't it?'

'That's right,' said Ben. 'She loved it.'

'It's my garden now,' said Colin. 'I like it. I shall come here every day. But that must be a secret. No one must know that we come here. Mary and Dickon have worked and made it come alive. We'll ask you to come and help sometimes. But you must come secretly, when no one can see you.'

Ben's face twisted into a dry old smile.

'I've come secretly before,' he said. 'She liked this garden so much, your mother. She asked me to look after it for her. So after she died, I came and did a bit of work for her every year. But I didn't come through the door. I came over the wall.'

'That's why so many roses are still alive,' said Dickon. 'I thought someone had done some work here.'

Dickon had left a trowel[77] lying on the grass near the tree, and Colin suddenly reached out and picked it up. He had a strange look on his face, and he started digging at the earth. His hand was weak. But as they watched him, he dug the trowel into the earth and turned some over.

'You said I'd walk like other people,' he said excitedly to Dickon. 'And you said I'd dig. This is only the first day, and I've walked. And now I'm digging!'

'Would you like to plant something, Master Colin?' Ben Weatherstaff asked. 'I could get you a rose in a pot.'

'Go and get it!' said Colin, digging happily. 'Quick! Quick!'

Ben Weatherstaff hurried away to find the rose. Dickon took his spade and helped Colin make the hole deeper.

'I want to do it before the sun goes down,' said Colin, looking up at the sky.

When Ben came back, Colin put the rose into the hole. Ben and Dickon helped him fill the rose in and press it down.

'It's planted!' said Colin at last. 'Help me up, Dickon. I want to stand up and watch the sun going down.'

Dickon helped Colin up. And when the sun finally went down at the end of that strange and lovely afternoon, Colin was standing on his two feet laughing.

11

'I am Getting Stronger!'

The next few months in the garden were like magic[78]. At first there were green shoots coming up everywhere – in the grass, in the flowerbeds and even on the walls. Then the buds appeared. And then the buds opened out and the garden was full of colour. The poppies Dickon and Mary had planted grew, and the roses covered the garden. They climbed the walls, hung from the trees and grew out of the grass. They seemed to come alive every minute, and their smell filled the garden air.

Colin saw it all. He spent every hour of each day in the garden. He watched things growing. He watched the insects and birds in the garden. And he learned from Dickon about other animals, too. Suddenly he had a whole new world to discover.

Because he had stood on his feet, Colin had something else new to think about too. He wanted to walk and run, and he wanted to be as strong as Dickon. So every morning, with Mary standing on one side, and Dickon on the other, he walked around the garden. The first time, they had to stop after every few steps, and Colin held on to Dickon's arm. But sometimes Colin took his arm away, put his head up high, and walked a few steps alone.

'I am getting stronger! I can feel it!' he cried, after they had walked all around the garden for the first time.

'What will Dr Craven say?' cried Mary, excited.

'He won't know,' Colin answered. 'This is going to be the biggest secret of all. No one will know about it. I don't want my father to hear about it. We'll wait until I can walk and run like other boys. Then when my father comes back to Misselthwaite, I shall walk into his room. And I shall say, "Here I am. I am quite well and I shall live to be a man."'

'He won't believe his eyes!' cried Mary.

Colin's cheeks were red. He finally believed that he was going to get well. And he couldn't wait to show his father that he was as straight and as strong as any other boy.

But it was difficult for the children to keep their secret. Each day Colin grew a little stronger. He no longer looked like a sick child. His skin now had a warm colour, his beautiful eyes were clear, and he was starting to get fatter. He and Mary were always hungry now. After every meal, their plates were empty. The children knew that the servants were starting to wonder why Master Colin was suddenly eating so much. So the children decided they must try to eat less. But every morning, they woke up feeling hungry. And when they saw their breakfast laid out, they could never send it away.

The children had decided that Dickon's mother could know their secret. They all agreed that she would never tell anyone. So one beautiful evening, while Dickon was working in his vegetable garden at home, he told her the whole story. He told her about the buried key, and the garden, and about Master Colin getting stronger.

'My word!' she said, when he had finished talking. 'It's a good thing that little girl came to the Manor. It's been good for her, and it's saved Master Colin. You say he stood on his feet! And we all thought he was a poor crooked boy. What do they think of it all at the Manor?'

'They can't understand it,' laughed Dickon. 'Master Colin's keeping it all a secret. He doesn't want them to write and tell his father. So he pretends he's still ill. When the servants carry him down to the wheelchair, he lies back like a sick child, moaning[79] and complaining. The problem is that Master Colin and Miss Mary are always hungry now. They want to ask for more food. But they know the servants won't believe Master Colin is still ill!'

Dickon's mother laughed.

'Oh, they're enjoying themselves, aren't they!' she said. 'I'll tell you what, son. In the morning, I'll bake them some nice bread, and you can take them some fresh milk. That will stop them feeling hungry!'

'Oh, Mother! You are wonderful!' cried Dickon. 'What a good idea!'

And so the next morning, after the children had been in the garden for a while, Dickon brought out a bucket of milk and some fresh bread, still warm. Mary and Colin were delighted.

'Your mother is such a kind, clever woman, Dickon!' they cried. 'The milk is so good! And the bread is wonderful!'

12

Mr Craven Comes Home

While the secret garden was coming alive, and two children were coming alive with it, Mr Archie Craven was travelling around beautiful places in Europe. His mind had been full of dark, sad thoughts for ten years. Something terrible had happened to him when he had been happy. And he had refused to let any light into his life since then. But slowly – slowly – as he walked among beautiful mountains and wandered by blue lakes, he began to grow stronger.

Mr Craven began to think about Misselthwaite Manor, and wondered if he should go home. Sometimes he thought about his son. He wondered how he would feel when he looked at Colin's white face once more. He felt frightened when he thought about it.

One beautiful day, Mr Craven went out walking all day. When he came back to the house where he was staying, the moon was high in the sky. The lake near the house was so still in the silver moonlight that he walked down and sat on a seat near the water. He breathed in the lovely smells of the night, and felt strangely calm. He felt calmer and calmer, until at last he fell asleep.

And as he slept, he dreamed a dream that seemed very real. It seemed so real that he wasn't even sure he had been dreaming. In his dream, he heard a sweet happy voice, calling to him from far away.

'Archie! Archie!' the voice said.

It was the voice of his dead wife.

'Lilias!' he cried out to her. 'Where are you?'

'In the garden,' she answered. 'In the garden!'

That was the end of Mr Craven's dream, but he did not wake up. He slept deeply all night, on the seat by the lake. When he woke, it was morning, and a servant was standing in front of him, holding a letter.

Mr Craven took the letter, and sat staring at the lake for a few moments. He was remembering his dream.

'In the garden,' he said to himself. 'But the door is locked and the key is buried.'

When he looked at the letter a few minutes later, he saw that it had come from Yorkshire. He opened the letter and read it.

Dear Sir,

I am Susan Sowerby, Martha's mother. I spoke to you about Miss Mary a little while ago when I met you in Thwaite. I would like to speak to you about something else. Please, sir, I think you should come home. I think you will be pleased that you have come back. And I think your wife would ask you to come if she was here.

Kind regards,
Susan Sowerby

Mr Craven read the letter twice, and then put it down. He kept thinking about the dream.

'I will go back to Misselthwaite,' he said to himself. 'I'll go straight away.'

And he went back to the house and told the servants to get ready to go back to England.

On the way back to Yorkshire, he thought a lot about his son, Colin. When his wife had died, he had been like a madman. He had been angry because his wife was dead and his son was alive. He had not felt like a father at all. He had gone away travelling. And when he came back and saw his son, he could not look at him. Colin's eyes were so like his wife's happy eyes, and yet so different from them, because they were so sad. After that, he only went to see Colin when he was asleep. The servants told him that Colin was sick, and that he had big tantrums.

Mr Craven kept remembering the voice he had heard in his dream: '*In the garden, in the garden*'.

'I will try to find the key,' he said to himself. 'I will try to open the door. I must – although I don't know why.'

When Mr Craven arrived back at Misselthwaite Manor, he went straight out into the gardens. The flower beds were full of autumn flowers and the fountain was playing. Without knowing why, he walked across the lawn and down to the long walk at the back of the secret garden. When he got there, he wondered if he was dreaming again. There was thick ivy over the door still. But he could hear noises inside the garden. He could hear the noise of quiet laughter, and running feet. He could hear someone running faster and faster. And then suddenly the door in the wall flew open, and a boy ran out very fast, straight into Mr Craven's arms.

Mr Craven held the boy away from him and looked at him, amazed. He was a tall handsome boy and his face was full of colour. When Mr Craven saw his eyes, he gasped. They were full of laughter.

This was not how Colin had planned to meet his father. He had come running out of the garden because he had just won a race with Mary and Dickon. But in fact, it was probably the best possible way of surprising Mr Craven.

'Father,' he said, 'I'm Colin. You can't believe it, I know. The garden made me well. Aren't you glad, Father? I'm going to live for ever and ever and ever!'

Mr Craven was trembling with happiness. He put his hands on the boy's shoulders and held him still. He couldn't speak for a moment.

A boy ran out very fast, straight into Mr Craven's arms.

'Take me into the garden, my boy,' he said at last. 'And tell me all about it.'

Mary and Dickon had run out of the garden after Colin, and together they all led Mr Craven back inside. The garden was full of autumn colour – gold and purple and red – and late roses climbed and hung all around. Mr Craven looked round and round.

'I thought it would be dead,' he said.

'That was what Mary thought too,' said Colin. 'But it came alive.'

Then they sat down under the tree, and the children told him their story. They told him how Mary and Colin had met in the middle of the night. They told him about the spring coming, and about their great secret. Mr Craven laughed until he cried, and sometimes he cried when he was not laughing.

'Now,' said Colin, at the end of the story, 'it doesn't have to be a secret any more. I am never going to go in the wheelchair again. I shall walk back with you to the house, Father.'

A few minutes later, Mrs Medlock was looking out of the kitchen window when she gave a little cry. All the servants came running over, and looked out with her.

Mr Craven, the Master of Misselthwaite, was walking across the garden towards them, looking happier than he had been for years. And next to him, his head up in the air, and his eyes full of laughter, was Master Colin. Walking as strongly as any boy in Yorkshire!

Points for Understanding

1

1 Why did Mary Lennox go to live in Yorkshire?
2 Describe Mary's character at the beginning of the story.
3 Why did Mrs Medlock think that Mr Craven would not look after Mary?

2

1 Why was Martha surprised when Mary did not eat her breakfast?
2 When was one of the gardens locked up?
3 Where did Mary first see the robin?

3

1 Why did Mr Craven hate the locked garden?
2 What did Mary hear when she was with Martha?
3 Where did Mary find the key to the secret garden?

4

1 Why had Mary not been able to find the door to the secret garden before?
2 What work did Mary do in the secret garden on her first visit?
3 Why did Martha and Mary write a letter to Dickon?

5

1 Who taught Ben Weatherstaff about roses?
2 How did Mary know that Dickon would keep her secret?
3 Why did Dickon think that someone had been into the secret garden in the last ten years?
4 What did Mary ask Mr Craven for?

6

1 Why did Colin think that he was going to die?
2 Colin wanted to tell his servants to open up the secret garden. Why did Mary try to stop him?

7

1 Why was Martha surprised that Colin had been nice to Mary?
2 In what ways did Mary think that Colin was different from Dickon?
3 Why did not Mary tell Colin that she had been into the secret garden?

8

1 Why did Mary and Dickon want Colin to come into the secret garden?
2 Why was Colin angry with Mary?

9

1 What gifts did Mr Craven send Mary?
2 Which animals did Dickon bring to see Colin?

10

1 Why was Mrs Medlock surprised that Colin wanted to go into the gardens?
2 Why did Ben Weatherstaff cry when he saw Colin?
3 Why had Ben come into the garden secretly before?

11

1 Why didn't Colin want Dr Craven to know that he could walk?
2 Why did Dickon's mother give the children milk and bread?

12

1. What were the two reasons why Mr Craven decided to come back to Misselthwaite Manor?
2. Why did Mr Craven think that he was dreaming when he stood outside the secret garden?

Glossary

1 **empire** (page 5)
a number of countries that are ruled by one person or government.

2 **servant** (page 5)
someone whose job is to cook, clean, or do other work in someone else's home.

3 **manor** (page 5)
a large house with a lot of land and small buildings around it.

4 **cholera** (page 7)
a serious disease that affects your stomach and the tubes in your body that process food and carry waste out of your body.

5 **selfish** (page 7)
thinking only about yourself and not caring about other people.

6 **disagreeable** (page 7)
not friendly or polite.

7 **hunchback** (page 7)
an offensive word for someone who has a large round part on their back.

8 **delightful** (page 8)
very nice.

9 **housekeeper** (page 8)
someone whose job is to clean or cook in a large house or a hotel.

10 **messily** (page 8)
in a dirty or very untidy way.

11 **spoilt** (page 9)
a spoilt child behaves badly if they do not get what they want. This is because people have always given them everything that they want. Mrs Medlock thinks that Mary looks like a spoilt child.

12 **gloomy** (page 9)
a place that is *gloomy* is dark in a way that makes you feel sad or a little afraid. When a person is *gloomy* they are feeling sad and without hope.

13 **moor** (page 9)
a large area of high land that is covered with grass, bushes, and small plants. It has soil that is not good for growing crops.

14 **crooked** (page 9)
not straight.

15 **carriage** (page 10)
a vehicle pulled by horses, used in the past for carrying passengers.

16 **curious** (page 10)
wanting to find out about something.

17 **heather** (page 10)
heather is a plant with small purple or white flowers which grows wild in the countryside of Europe.

18 **gorse** (page 10)
gorse is a small bush with yellow flowers and sharp points that stick out from the stem. Gorse also grows wild in the countryside in Europe.

19 **ponies** – *pony* (page 10)
a small horse.

20 **corridor** (page 11)
a long passage inside a building with doors on each side.

21 **robin redbreast** (page 11)
a robin is a small brown European bird. The front part of its body, which is called its *breast*, is red. Robins are also called *robin redbreasts*.

22 **humming** – *to hum* (page 12)
to make a low continuous sound.

23 **accent** (page 12)
a way of pronouncing words that shows what country, region, or social class you come from.

24 **disobeyed** – *to disobey* (page 13)
to deliberately not pay attention to a rule or an order from someone in authority.

25 **sorry** – *to feel sorry for somebody* (page 13)
to feel sympathy for someone because they are in a difficult or unpleasant situation.

26 **relieved** (page 13)
happy and relaxed because something bad has ended or did not happen.

27 **chattered** – *to chatter* (page 13)
to talk in a fast informal way about unimportant subjects.

28 **foxes** – *fox* (page 14)
a wild animal similar to a small dog, with red-brown fur and a thick tail. A young *fox* is called a *fox cub*.

29 **bare** (page 15)
a bare surface has nothing on it. The garden is *bare* because there are no flowers in it.

30 **buried** – *to bury something* (page 15)
to put something in the ground and cover it with earth.
31 **lawn** (page 15)
an area of grass that is cut short, especially in a garden.
32 **fountain** (page 15)
a *fountain* is a stream of water which is sent up into the air. It is a decoration for gardens and streets.
33 **orchard** (page 15)
a place where fruit trees are grown.
34 **digging** – *to dig* (page 17)
to make a hole in earth using your hands, a machine, or a tool.
35 **whistled** – *to whistle* (page 17)
to make a high sound by forcing air through your lips.
36 **hopped** – *to hop* (page 17)
if a bird or animal hops, it uses both or all four feet to jump forward.
37 **realized** – *to realize* (page 17)
to gradually begin to understand something that you did not know or notice before.
38 **temper** (page 18)
a tendency to get angry very quickly.
39 **spade** (page 18)
a tool used for digging that consists of a handle and a flat part that you push into the earth.
40 **ivy** (19)
a dark green plant that spreads and grows up walls.
41 **twitter** (page 20)
a high singing sound that is made by a bird.
42 **branch** (page 21)
one of the parts of a tree that grows out of its *trunk* (= its main stem).
43 **fox cub** (page 22)
a young wild animal similar to a small dog, with red-brown fur, a pointed face and a thick tail.
44 **crow** (page 22)
a large black bird that makes a loud sound.
45 **crocuses and snowdrops and daffodils** (page 22)
a *crocus* is a small yellow, white, or purple flower. *Snowdrops* are a type of small white flower. *Daffodils* are tall yellow flowers. These flowers all start to appear in early spring. They are a sign that the winter has ended.

46 ***trembled*** – *to tremble* (page 23)
if you are trembling, your body is shaking, for example because you are nervous or weak.

47 ***knob*** (page 25)
a round handle on a door or drawer.

48 ***mysterious*** (page 25)
not explained, understood, or known.

49 ***shoot*** (page 27)
a very young plant, or a new part growing on a plant.

50 ***weed*** (page 27)
a wild plant that grows in places where you do not want it.

51 ***plant*** (page 28)
to put trees, plants, or seeds in soil so that they will grow there.

52 ***seed*** (page 28)
a small hard part produced by a plant that can grow into a new plant of the same type.

53 ***lump*** (page 29)
a solid piece that does not have a regular shape on a surface that should be smooth.

54 ***pipe*** (page 30)
a musical instrument with one or more tubes that you blow through.

55 ***squirrel*** (page 30)
a grey or red-brown animal with a long thick tail. Squirrels live in trees.

56 ***nest*** (page 32)
a structure that birds make to keep their eggs and babies in.

57 ***thrush*** (page 34)
a brown bird with light spots on its breast.

58 ***miserable*** (page 34)
extremely unhappy.

59 ***gasped*** – *to gasp* (page 38)
to breathe in suddenly because you are surprised, shocked, or in pain.

60 ***wheelchair*** (page 42)
a chair with large wheels that someone who cannot walk uses for moving around.

61 ***tantrum*** (page 44)
an occasion when someone, especially a young child, suddenly behaves in a very angry way that is unreasonable or silly.

62 **medicine** (page 44)
a substance that you take to treat an illness.
63 **mood** (page 44)
the way that someone is feeling at a particular time. If someone is *in a good mood*, they are happy and relaxed. If someone is *in a bad mood*, they are unhappy or angry.
64 **dressing gown** (page 45)
a piece of clothing like a long loose coat that you wear in your house.
65 **leaf-bud** (page 48)
a part of a plant that opens to form a leaf.
66 **beak** (page 48)
the hard curved or pointed part of a bird's mouth.
67 **mate** (page 48)
an animal's sexual partner.
68 **choked** – *to choke* (page 50)
if someone chokes, or chokes up, they cannot speak clearly because they are starting to cry.
69 **lamb** (page 53)
a young sheep.
70 **patch** (page 56)
an area that is different from what surrounds it. The *patches* of colour are the flowers that are appearing in the garden.
71 **fluttering** – *to flutter* (page 56)
to move with quick light movements, or to make something move in this way.
72 **blossom** (57)
a flower on a tree, or all the flowers on a tree.
73 **flash** (page 57)
a bright light or colour that appears for a very short time.
74 **ladder** (page 58)
a piece of equipment for reaching high places. It has two long pieces of wood or metal joined by smaller pieces called rungs.
75 **fist** (page 58)
your hand when your fingers are closed tightly.
76 **rug** (page 58)
a cloth made of wool that you use to keep yourself warm.
77 **trowel** (page 61)
a small tool with a curved blade that is used in gardens for digging.

78 **magic** (page 62)
a mysterious power that makes impossible things happen if you do special actions or say special words.

79 **moaning** – *to moan* (page 64)
to complain about something in an annoying way.

Exercises

Vocabulary: meanings of words from the story

Put the words and phrases in the box next to the correct meanings.

crooked branch bury gloomy disagreeable crow moan flutter disobey choke mood lawn gasp relieved miserable nest lump seed mysterious knob tremble spade temper selfish whistle patch bare corridor curious fountain medicine moor spoilt robin servant carriage dig fox plant weed

1		1 not pleasant or enjoyable 2 not friendly or polite
2		thinking only about yourself and not caring about other people
3		1 to make a long, low sound 2 to complain in an annoying way
4		to move up and down or from side to side with short, quick, light movements – a flag in the wind / a bird's wings / falling leaves
5		a piece of ground, especially one where you grow fruit or vegetables
6		be unable to breathe because something is blocking your throat
7		the way someone is feeling, for example whether they are happy, sad, or angry
8		something that you take to treat an illness – pills, tablets, etc.
9		to breathe in suddenly because you are surprised, shocked, or in pain
10		extremely unhappy or uncomfortable

11		a structure that birds make to keep their eggs and babies in
12		a solid piece of something that does not have a regular shape
13		a small hard part produced by a plant, which can grow into a new plant of the same type
14		a living thing that grows in soil, has leaves and roots, and needs water and light from the sun to live
15		a plant that grows easily in places where you do not want it
16		not explained or understood
17		a round handle on a door or drawer
18		to shake because you are nervous, afraid, excited, or cold
19		a large black bird that makes a loud sound
20		a part of a tree that grows out of its main body
21		a tool used for digging earth
22		a tendency to get angry very quickly
23		the sound someone makes when they force air through their lips
24		an area of grass that is cut short, especially in a garden or park
25		a structure through which a stream of water is pumped into the air and falls down again
26		1 surfaces that have no covering or decoration – walls / floors, etc. 2 empty – when there is nothing inside a cupboard or refrigerator, etc.
27		to do the opposite of what someone tells you to do deliberately

28		a long passage inside a building with doors on each side
29		wanting to find out about something
30		not straight
31		a large area of high land covered with grass, bushes, and heather, with soil that is not good for growing crops
32		dark in a way that makes you feel sad or a little afraid
33		a child who behaves badly when she does not get what she wants
34		a small brown European bird with a red chest
35		someone whose job is to cook, clean, or do other work in someone else's home
36		a vehicle with wheels that is pulled by horses, especially one used in the past before cars were invented
37		to make a hole in earth or sand
38		a wild animal similar to a small dog, with red-brown fur, a pointed face, and a thick tail
39		happy and relaxed because something bad has not happened, or because a bad situation has ended
40		to put something in the ground and cover it with dirt

Writing: rewrite sentences

Rewrite the sentences using words and phrases in the previous exercise to replace the underlined words.

Example:	*Mary was <u>unpleasant and impolite</u>.*
You write:	*Mary was disagreeable.*

1 Mary <u>only thought about herself</u>.

2 Colin takes <u>too many pills</u>.

3 His face was <u>extremely unhappy</u>.

4 Colin thought that there was a <u>strange shape growing</u> on his back.

5 There was an <u>area of ground</u> where roses grew.

6 Mary cut the <u>unwanted plants</u> around the roses.

7 Mary saw a door <u>handle</u> underneath the leaves.

8 I would like a <u>tool</u> to dig in the garden.

9 There was a <u>wide area of grass</u> in the middle of the garden.

10 The garden had no flowers: it looked <u>empty</u>.

11 Mr Craven's back was <u>not straight</u>.

12 They travelled to the old house in a vehicle pulled by horses.

13 He locked the door and hid the key in the ground.

14 Mary stopped crying and Martha looked more relaxed.

15 She led Mary down a long passageway with doors on either side.

16 Colin's hand shook.

17 She saw a black bird land on top of the wall.

18 And all around them they heard birds moving their wings.

19 In India, Mary was looked after by employees in her parents' house.

20 It was a bird sitting on a place which it had made for its eggs.

21 Dickon lived in a cottage on the bare land covered with grass and heather.

22 She wanted to know where they were going.

Vocabulary and Grammar: look / feel / sound

In the story, how did these people *look* or *feel* or *sound*? Or what did the places look like? Rewrite the sentences using the words look, feel or sound.

Example: *Martha had a cheerful face.*
You write: *Martha looked cheerful.*

1 Mary was always bad-tempered and frowned most of the time.

2 The garden was dull because it had no flowers.

3 The moor was flat. It reminded Mary of a dark sea.

4 The gardener did not have a friendly face.

5 Mary did not have any friends. 'I'm lonely,' she said.

6 The robin was whistling happily.

7 My father does not like to see me. I make him miserable.

8 He spoke in an angry way.

9 The big garden was tidy. The secret garden was in a mess.

10 Mary's face had a healthy colour.

Vocabulary and Grammar: fill in the gaps

Complete the story using words from the box. There are two extra words.

teachers at her she but mother and to servants when old sickness friends heard after eat go stood was opened another child were who because everything must hid left doorway dead morning bury crying came always spade not water looked place nobody

Mary Lennox was a sickly child. She lived in India and she was [1] .... sick. Her hair was yellow, [2] .... skin was yellow and [3] .... had a very bad temper.

Nobody liked Mary Lennox. [4] .... came to the house to teach her, [5] .... they did not stay [6] .... Mary was rude. Her [7] .... and father did not like her [8] .... they did not talk [9] .... her. They told their British [10] ....: 'Our daughter is sick. She [11] .... stay in the house in the garden. The [12] .... can look after her.'

There [13] .... many servants in the house. They looked after Mary but Mary was always angry and shouted [14] .... them: 'Sons of pigs! Daughters of pigs! Do this! Do that!' The servants did [15] .... disobey young Mary. They did [16] .... that Mary wanted.

One day, [17] .... Mary was nine years [18] .... , everything changed. There was [19] .... in the town and sickness [20] .... to her parents' house. Mary [21] .... people crying. The servants were [22] .... Nobody came to look [23] .... her. She was afraid.

She [24] .... in the house in the garden for two days and waited and listened. She drank a little [25] .... but did not want to [26] .... She did not want to [27] .... outside. Then, on the third [28] .... , there was silence.

Mary [29] .... in the middle of the room. She [30] .... hungry and angry and afraid. She [31] .... small and ugly, when the door [32] ....

A British officer and [33] .... soldier stood in the [34] .... The officer looked astonished. 'There is a [35] .... here! A child alone! In a [36] .... like this! Mercy on us, [37] .... is she?'

'I am Mary Lennox,' said Mary.

'She is the child who [38] .... ever saw,' said the soldier. 'And now there is nobody [39] .... in the house to look after her. They are all [40] ....'

Vocabulary: anagrams

The letters of each word are mixed up. Write the words correctly.

Example:

TELLIT	*She had a thin face and body.*
You write:	*She had a thin little face and body.*

1	NIGBOWL	Is that the sound of the wind?
2	FLYEROUS	'Can't you dress?' she asked.
3	CODELK	She kept thinking about the garden.
4	DULENDSY	The gardener smiled.
5	RONDIOS	There was nothing for her to do.
6	CERTES	Mary began to feel very interested in the garden.
7	DOWNOE	A boy was sitting under a tree, playing on a pipe.

8	DALERAY	Perhaps everything in it is dead.
9	TUODIES	You can play as much as you like.

Grammar: syntax

Put the words into the correct order to make sentences.

Example: *She told the secret him about all garden.*
You write: *She told him all about the secret garden.*

1 I'm afraid to shake my legs because so much stand up.

2 before he had made His anger stronger than him ever been.

3 They never agreed that all she would tell anyone.

4 Mr Craven heard in his dream the voice he had kept remembering.

5 He was full of boy and a tall handsome face was his colour.

6 The hand fell on Colin's face with a touch like a lovely sun.

7 He's flying up in the sky always looking to watch birds.

8 The fresh air was blue, and the moor that blew in was warm.

Macmillan Education Limited
4 Crinan Street
London N1 9XW

Companies and representatives throughout the world

Macmillan Readers Pre-Intermediate Secret Garden, The
ISBN: 978-1-035-15053-3
Macmillan Readers Pre-Intermediate Secret Garden, The with eBook and Resources
ISBN: 978-1-035-15062-5

This is a retold version by Rachel Bladon of the original work by Frances Hodgson Burnett.

First published 2008
This version published 2024

Illustrated by Janos Jantner
Cover photograph by Getty/theasis

Printed and bound in Brazil

2025
12